The Names of Things

The Names of Things

NEW AND SELECTED POEMS

Jeffrey Harrison

WAYWISER

First published in 2006 by

THE WAYWISER PRESS

9 Woodstock Road, London N4 3ET, UK
P.O. Box 6205, Baltimore, MD 21206, USA
www.waywiser-press.com

Managing Editor
Philip Hoy

Associate Editors
Joseph Harrison   Clive Watkins   Greg Williamson

A CIP catalogue record for this book is available from the British Library

ISBN-10: 1-904130-20-8
ISBN-13: 978-1-904130-20-8

Printed and bound by
Cromwell Press Ltd., Trowbridge, Wiltshire

For Julie, William, and Eliza

Acknowledgements

The poems in this volume were taken from the following books, whose publishers the author wishes to thank:

The Singing Underneath (E.P. Dutton), © 1988 by Jeffrey Harrison. Used with permission of the author.

Signs of Arrival (Copper Beech Press), © 1996 by Jeffrey Harrison. Used with permission of the author.

Feeding the Fire (Sarabande Books), © 2001 by Jeffrey Harrison. Used with permission of the publisher, Sarabande Books, Inc., Louisville, Kentucky.

Incomplete Knowledge (Four Way Books), © 2006 Jeffrey Harrison. Used with permission of the publisher, Four Way Books, Inc., New York. All rights reserved.

*

In addition, grateful acknowledgement is made to the editors of the following publications in which the newer poems first appeared: *The Missouri Review*: "Visitation"; *The Paris Review*: "Saint"; *The Southern Review*: "His Socks" (from "An Undertaking"); *The Yale Review*: "Fork," "The Names of Things."

"Saint," "Visitation," and "His Socks" also appeared in the chapbook *An Undertaking* (Haven Street Press, 2005).

*

I am grateful to the following people for their suggestions and help with the manuscript: Karen Chase, Robert Cording, Alan Feldman, Jessica Greenbaum, Eric Karpeles, Peter Schmitt, and Charlie Worthen.

Contents

Contents

from The Singing Underneath (1988)

The Singing Underneath

The sun comes up, steam rises
from the field, and the ice-glazed trees
begin to drip. A few prismatic drops

quiver on the branches like tiny,
fidgeting birds. No, more like
a visual singing of birds: as if

just underneath the world we see,
there is a silent singing that breaks out
at moments, in flickering points of light.

Canoeing with My Brother

for Jeremy

A bullfrog's low reverberation
draws us toward the inkblot of the shore.
Nothing has changed since we were boys:
the beam of the flashlight in the mist
bounces off the water, up into the trees,
then spotlights him, a paddle's length away,

a Buddha on a heart-shaped lily pad.
Though he's been calling for a mate all night,
his eyes are absent of desire. The light
spreads through his limbs, paralyzing him,
except his throat, which pulses slightly.
His milky belly bulges against the leaf.

Years ago, we would have smacked him with a paddle
and later cut his legs off, peeling the skin
from braided flesh, like long green rubber gloves –
white and red-veined as they turned inside out
down to the tips of the long, bony toes.
These legs he would have died for

are folded into compact Z's. His arms
look atrophied, vestigial in contrast,
the hands turned inward like the hands
of an aikido master or someone
in a Japanese tea ceremony
"sitting seiza," just about to bow.

Another frog, nearby, starts bellowing.
"He'll never do it with us next to him,"
my brother whispers. But just then
his throat swells bigger than a chicken egg,
and with no change of expression,
with no expression at all, he starts to sing.

The Hummingbird Feeder

If what we wait to see partly defines us,
then this red bulb hanging in the blue
is a simple model for the heart,
swaying slightly at the end of its string
as I rock slightly, standing next to it,
eyes fixed, waiting for the buzz, the blur
of wings, the body like a tiny seal's
balancing the feeder on its nose.

Surely these moments we stand on tiptoe for
make us what we are as much as pain
and sorrow: the moment the hummingbird
flashes his red throat, the moment he spreads
his tail and swerves off like a fish, a green
streak, then sticks like a leaf to a branch –
the moment he stops in midair and sticks
his beak into that severed artery.

As he drinks, an embolism forms,
like the bubble in a spirit level,
and rises slowly up the tube, a bit
of the outside world going in, a moment
trapped: like one of those clear marbles
in which everything is upside-down, and small.
As the last drop quivers and disappears
with the bird, the heart becomes a mind.

In the Attic

The thick air smelled of dust and wood.
Shiny, blue-black wasps, dangling their legs,
bounced off the facets of the roof
with quick, electrical buzzes.
I used to stay up there for hours, sitting
on the rough floor, jagged with splinters,

paging through stacks of *Life* magazine.
Or I'd stare through the Gothic window,
past spider webs, dead wasps,
and the ragged nests the starlings
had stuffed into the bargeboard, to feel
what it's like to be in the treetops.

This time I was up there for a reason.
Years before, in the top drawer of a dresser
my mother had painted Pennsylvania Dutch,
I'd found a bundle of envelopes
stained amber by the attic's heat
like the mattresses piled on the old brass bed.

I'd been afraid to read them. Now,
I untied the dull blue ribbon.
It stayed crimped and folded from the bow.
The yellow pages crackled as I opened them.
They were written by my father, full of
ambition, jealousy, infatuation.

It was a side of him I'd never seen.
I had written letters like these
when I was fourteen, letters I'd burn
to see now. I read each one, one for every
day that summer. There was one from my mother:
blue ink on white paper, no envelope.

She described a view I knew by heart:
the lake framed by hemlocks, the mountain
reflected in the evening, its rock face
staring blankly. She said it made her think
of God. She said, yes, she would be his wife
if he was sure he understood what that meant.

Country Wedding

After two days of rain, the sun
came out, miraculously, at four,
and the birds began to sing like crazy.

The guests assembled in the orchard
where a harp and flute were playing.
A rooster in the barnyard crowed

and the procession began:
squelching footsteps in the muddy aisle –
the maid of honor almost lost a shoe.

The music stopped. The minister intoned,
"We are gathered here to celebrate ..."
Two swallows, glinting blue, performed

acrobatic feats above the scene,
fluttering together for a moment
like the doves on willowware.

A bedraggled English setter sniffed its way
up the aisle and sat down by the bride:
an emblem of faithfulness, perhaps,

or beauty, since its name was Belle.
The sun shone brighter for the vows,
two ducks flew overhead just as the bride

and bridegroom kneeled, and the rooster
crowed again on the word *truth*
from chapter thirteen of Corinthians.

Near the end, I heard a distant siren;
then the dogs began to bark,
the geese to honk, the ducks to quack.

Country Wedding

Six buzzards circled overhead, the late sun
shining on their bladelike underwings,
then glided out of sight behind the hill.

Skating in Late Afternoon

As I step off the end of the dock, the dog
barks, a crack ricochets through the ice
like a vibration through a taut cable,
and I am eleven again, taking the first
tentative, gliding steps over the frozen pond.

Everyone has left. I am alone, afraid
of falling through, but soon I'm tracing
someone else's figure eight, then following
my own haphazard course over the black ice,
listening to the scraping of my skate blades.

As the sun goes down, the cedars on the hill
flare like green candle flames. They are
the dead: planted there a century ago
over victims of the plague,
by now completely taken up into their branches.

Each time I swing around toward them,
they've filled a little more with shadow,
until the last orange light breaks off the tips
into invisibility – as if their souls
were burning off so they could sleep.

Dark presences – they seem, now that I have become
aware of them, to be aware of me.

Slaughter Cows

A crowd of black faces, almost angry
despite their long eyelashes, moves toward me.
Numbered tags are stapled to their ears,
as if a lottery decides which ones

will die. Their noses glimmer, their nostrils
wide as the eye sockets of human skulls.
Flies land on the swirls of their foreheads
and gather at the dark pools of their eyes

to drink. The globs of dried mud in their tails
clack like wooden beads. Some of them lose
interest in me and start to walk away.
They breathe heavily, feeding, their dewlaps

swaying. I hold out a tuft of grass,
leaning against barbed wire, but they won't take it.
One climbs another's back, then falls away.
One drinks another's piss. They are full

of death. One has my death-age in its ear.

Poem

Like those spider webs strung across a path,
you don't see them until you're right on them
or until it's too late and you feel one
tickling your face – it breaks, the spider
scrambles up a strand onto a leaf,
and you go on, trailing a few new gray hairs.

Then you try to look out for them and maybe
sing a song about them to yourself
so as not to forget, but eventually
the song becomes just song, your thoughts
go out into your surroundings,
and before you can do anything about it,
you've broken another web just where
the trail opens into a field of goldenrod.

Trading the Alps for the Andes

Sometimes you meet an older person
whose vigor seems to mock your youth.
Like my grandfather – at ninety,
he still walks for miles in the woods
and dislodges boulders from the road.
Or like my great aunt Teeny, who
picked me up at the train station
in leather pants, having danced all night.
Or the Swiss woman we met in Peru
who was there to climb the highest peaks.
She'd come alone, leaving her husband
in a wheelchair by Lake Geneva.
She described the "little avalanche"
that had swept her down a mountain.
"Like swimming in a cloud," she said,
recommending the experience.
Just talking to her over dinner
was invigorating, a glimpse
of a future as bright as snowfields.
For now we'd settle for the foothills,
for alpine lakes of unreal blue,
for this firsthand account and a view
of the peaks – as jagged as chipped
obsidian, and white as it is black.

Butterflies

The rest-stops along the highway
are repetitions in a dream.
Time feels strange to us. We don't know
if it's morning or afternoon.
We drink the rusty water, stretch
our legs, eat at a picnic table,
then return to the blue Plymouth.
It is then that we notice them:
butterflies, flattened on the grille
as if a lepidopterist
had pinned them there. It is
a nice collection: two monarchs,
three small yellow ones, and a black
and yellow swallowtail with two
blue spots. Others are crumpled, torn
(like fragments of an image
inside a kaleidoscope),
or smashed into the radiator.
The car is like a whale that feeds
by sifting shrimp through its baleen
as it cruises on "the whale-road."
And like a whale it doesn't think
it shouldn't kill. It doesn't think
at all – we do. We think: *How
beautiful, this death.*
I try to peel one off
and burn my fingers.

Reflection on the Vietnam War Memorial

Here it is, the back porch of the dead.
You can see them milling around in there,
        screened in by their own names,
        looking at us in the same
vague and serious way we look at them.

An underground house, a roof of grass –
one version of the underworld. It's all
        we know of death: a world
        like our own (but darker, blurred),
inhabited by beings like ourselves.

The location of the name you're looking for
can be looked up in a book whose resemblance
        to a phone book seems to claim
        some contact can be made
through the simple act of finding a name.

As we touch the name the stone absorbs our grief.
It takes us in – we see ourselves inside it.
        And yet we feel it as a wall
        and realize the dead are all
just names now, the separation final.

The Light Cure

It doesn't matter where you are.
You will find it, when you need it,
at the end of day, in the intricate
flames of leafless trees, or the last light
climbing up a row of brownstones, getting
yellower, more tangible, but further,
until the cornices alone are glowing;
their chipped paint and ragged nests become
a glorious decay, the rich detail
of magical roofs above our drab world.
Even the matted feathers of the starlings
shine like birds of paradise. Crane your neck
for that moment when the light snaps
upward, the earth is buried, and everything
that matters dissolves into the sky,
because something in you may be lifted
or slightly pulled askew, as your body sinks.

The Otter in the Washington Zoo

is in love with a little girl.
Maybe it's because he's been
alone too long – or is it just
her red shirt he's attracted to?

She runs from one end to the other
of his window, and he follows,
swimming undulously, bubbles
trailing along his slick body.

She stops in the middle, and he
swerves to a halt, floating upright
with only his head above the water.
They are about the same size.

They stare into each other's eyes.
Then she ducks down, and he
dives to the bottom of the pool.
She is laughing and he is laughing bubbles.

The glass becomes a kind of mirror:
he returns her every movement with
a replica more graceful and alluring
to make her stay – leading her on

by following her lead. But now
her mother says it's time to go,
and she leaves him looking after her,
pawing lightly at the wall of glass.

Foxglove

Like fishmouths, the lower lip
protruding, the flowers open up
to take their one long breath,
and again the burly bumblebees
muscle their way into the caves
where their sweet, secret
rite takes place. Spires, bells,
spires of bells, it is the bees'
religion. Inside, the script
of desire – pink
freckles, the fine hair
of a girl's cheek, the curves
of stamens, like elaborate tusks –
draws them in. They stumble out
like drunken sailors, their forearms
heavy with nectar, pollen
stuck to their fuzz
like beer froth on a beard.

Clear Day

North wind today, the lake
rolls its thalo blue toward us
in steady waves and darker,
fanning gusts. The only
decisive wind we have, it
cleans up the sky, sweeps out
yesterday's clouds like clumps
of dust, and makes everything
crisp in its outline, just a bit
more real.

On hazy days,
the lake is a pale gray, just
like the sky, and the mountains
on the far shore, no longer
green but darker gray,
look like a strip of clouds,
as if the only view, framed
by hemlocks (moving their arms
slowly like underwater
plants), were sky.

Today,
the lake is just the lake (or
more the lake than ever, bluer),
the mountains are themselves
again, and the hemlocks are
gesticulating wildly
as if exhilarated by this
unambiguous view. Life
is seldom this clear, free
of illusion, even here
where we come to get away.

The One That Got Away

for Julie

We paddled through the winding waterway,
past lily pads and water hyacinths,
into the other lake: perfectly calm
and of a blue much deeper than usual.
It was that time of day when late sunlight
intensifies the beauty of everything,
transforming the trees into a green fire.
They leaned over us as we paddled by
as if with the desire to be draped
in undulating nets of yellow light
projected by the waves from our canoe –
waves in which those very trees were mirrored,
stretched and wavering. We drifted in silence.
The paddle that I held across my lap
dripped, as if to count the passing moments –
getting slower, but we knew they wouldn't stop.
And we knew those nets of light, unraveling
all the while, wouldn't catch the afternoon
for us to keep – though you turned to me and said
that this was all you wanted in the world.

from Signs of Arrival (1996)

Household Spirits

Halfway to heaven, high up on a pole,
and the pole planted firmly in the earth,
the martin house in my grandparents' back yard
came back to me on the earth's other side
when I saw the spirit houses in Thailand:
miniature shrines for household gods
placed on stands outside of every house
where the shadow of the house will never fall.
Astrologers determine the exact location
and the right time to perform the ceremony:
flowers are scattered and ritual waters poured
to appease the spirits thought to bring
happiness and prosperity to the household.
But if everything is not done properly
they can do evil and haunt the house itself.
"Good spirits will not live where there is dirt,"
a Shaker saying goes, and I remember
my grandfather telling me the birds
would refuse the house if it wasn't neat enough.
But they hadn't refused it, and a colony
of purple martins lived in the many compartments –
flighty utopians, the spirits of that farmhouse,
gathering overhead in buoyant swarms,
water in their voices, sky on their wings.

Totem

We had to rip a few boards
of the soffit off to fit
the new front door into place,
and when we stopped for lunch I stood
on a picnic bench and stuck
my head up through the opening,
into the stuffy darkness there
below the eaves and, as my eyes
adjusted, made it out – was that ...
a canoe paddle! – its wood
still golden under the varnish
when I pulled it into daylight
despite how many years
of lying completely enclosed
in that wedge of stale dark air.
That paddle had us baffled
until my mother remembered,
or thought she remembered, hearing
somewhere of a superstition
about a paddle in the roof
bringing good luck. The whole family
was there, as I remember,
standing on the cabin's porch,
and we passed the paddle from one
to another in amused wonder,
each member examining it
as if it were a talisman
or fetish and we were taking part
unwittingly in some ancient
but spontaneous ritual –
which is what it might have looked like
to anyone paddling by
on the lake below. At first
we wanted to keep it, but then
the fear of what dark current might

Totem

overtake our lives, an undertow
we were just beginning to feel,
outweighed the temptation to hang it
with the others in the boathouse.
So we slipped it through the hole
we'd made before nailing the boards
back where they belonged, closing it
in again, carrying on
the superstition or creating
a new one: a perfectly good
canoe paddle several feet
above our heads, steering us
through difficult passages
and blessing us each time
we pass underneath it,
going in or out the door.

Adirondack Moosehead

The moose that once presided over games
of Monopoly and crazy eights,
that loomed above us, goofy and majestic,
into whose antlers we threw paper planes,
still hangs over the great stone fireplace
like the figurehead of a ship.

All these years he hasn't flicked an eyelash
in response to anything we've done,
and in that way resembles God,
whom, as children, we imagined looking down
but didn't know how to visualize. A moose
over the altar would have been

as good as anything – better than a cross –
staring down on us with kind dark eyes
that would have seemed, at least, to understand,
his antlers like gigantic upturned hands
ready to lift us off the ground –
or like enormous wings outspread for flight.

Mayflies

Every day for a week we watch them,
appearing, as if out of nowhere,
on the lake's surface, each one
having risen as a nymph from the bottom
and hatched into a creature lovely enough
to make us stop rowing for a moment,
our raised oars dripping quietly.
Something about the graceful curve
of its abdomen, and its tail
of two fine filaments, like paintbrushes
for depicting the minutest details.
Something about its plight,
its lifespan of a single day, the way
it hardly stands a chance.
Borne on that perilous interface, it must
sit there, trembling, exposed from both sides
to annihilation, gather its tiny wits,
and wait for its delicate wings
to become firm enough for flight.
Those first flickering attempts
only serve to send out
rippled signals to the trout below,
one of which will suddenly
break the surface with a splash.
Or the blurred swerve of a swallow
will skim the lake and snatch the fly.
Sometimes the mayfly will escape
the surface tension, fluttering up
 – only to be picked off in midair.
Yet some of them must make it through.
By week's end there are hundreds, thousands,
and the flocks of blackbirds and waxwings
that have moved in from who knows where
madly lurch and dive but can't
get them all, so that a few

Mayflies

can dodge the birds and take the risk
of mating in flight, floating up in tandem
over the treetops at the lake's edge ...
Every year it happens like this,
the confetti of summer's arrival
swirling over the lake, this storm
of insects that is not a plague
but a sign as sure and startling
as winter's first snow, whose flakes
vanish one by one as they touch the lake.

Hitting Golfballs off the Bluff

They come back now, those nights my friend and I
hit golfballs off the bluff behind his house.
We were sixteen and had our learner's permits
but no girlfriends, unlike the football jocks
we couldn't stand but secretly envied.
Neither of us actually played golf,
but late one night we took his father's clubs
and started what became a ritual.
A Freudian would have a field day with it:
the clubs, the balls, the deep ravine below
with train tracks and a river running through it.
But for us it was pure exhilaration:
the sure feel of a good connection, zing
of the white ball disappearing into blackness,
then silence as we waited for the thud
against the ground below, splash in the river,
or bang against the roof of a freight car.
That drawn-out moment when we only listened,
holding our laughter back, seemed never-ending
and one time was: no sound came back at all,
as if we'd sent the golfball into orbit
like a new planet – one we might still see
moving across the sky on any night,
pocked like the moon, but smaller, shining green
with envy now, now deep red with desire.

Convenience Store

It was too late: the three of us were already
inside the glass door of the convenience store
when we noticed the man behind the counter
was our bulge-eyed biology teacher from ninth grade.
That face of a frog pickled in formaldehyde,
we'd have recognized it anywhere ... but here?
We would have given anything to disappear,
to avoid the situation, and avoid
having to imagine what had happened to him
in the few years since we'd left for college.
None of us imagined that in six years
I'd be teaching English to ninth graders
in a school much like the one we'd gone to,
and that I'd be so miserable doing it
I'd have to quit and take a low-pay job
as a guard in a museum, where I'd sit
reading a book, look up at Van Goghs and Bonnards
depicting places I would rather be,
or stare at the Rothkos until I was floating.
But back then we weren't prepared for any future
except one of effortless accomplishment,
as we weren't prepared for this encounter
and couldn't think of anything to do
except keep going toward the beer we'd come for
and carry it up to the counter, looking down
at the racks of candy as he rang it up.
Nobody said a thing. The silence stiffened
and divided us from him, until one of us –
the future investment banker in New York –
ruptured the invisible membrane by laughing
and making a comment I'm glad I can't recall.
Nor do I remember our teacher's reply,
only his inane smile, as if held by pins,
and what I now realize was sadness
swelling those eyes we thought were only comic –

Convenience Store

but we were already hustling toward the door
and out into the snow-plowed parking lot,
where a raw gust hit us flush in the face
and stuffed the breath back down our gulping throats.

Brief History of an Atlas

Printed in Spain in 1697,
with forty foldout maps tinted by hand,
leatherbound, it may have first been owned
by a merchant who fretted over the maps at night,
wondering what had happened to his ships.
The tiny galleons etched on the sea's grid
never moved, no matter how he stared,
and his ships never returned. His business collapsed,
and his property was auctioned in the public square.
But the atlas fell out of its wooden crate
and was picked up from the gutter by a peasant
whose wife used it as a cutting board for years,
webbing the leather cover with crisscrossed grooves
and impregnating it with the smell of onions
which, after a century, disappeared.

Meanwhile, during Napoleon's occupation
of Spain, beginning in 1808
and lasting only five years, a French soldier
had pilfered the atlas while raiding peasants' homes
and carried it across the Pyrenees.
Almost a century later, it turned up
in one of those Paris bookstalls along the Seine.
The maps were torn, the pages brown with age,
and silverfish had tunneled through the binding.
An American tourist bought it for a few francs
and brought it home. When he saw how the maps
fascinated the son of one of his friends,
he gave the atlas to the boy: my grandfather
at twelve years old, born almost exactly
two hundred years after the atlas was printed.

Last year, when he had just turned ninety-four,
I saw it on his shelf and took it down,
handling it like a priceless, ancient Bible.

"Oh, that old thing?" he said, and told me its story
as I turned the pages and unfolded the maps.
"I took it to a dealer once," he said.
"Completely worthless." But the maps still held
their tints, those galleons still sailed the seas,
the Russian steppe was covered with tiny trees,
and a spouting whale swam off the coast of Norway.
"It shows California as an island," he said,
then added nonchalantly, "You can have it,"
as if to say he was through with such nonsense
and would have no use for it anyway
in the terra incognita where he was going.

Two Salutations

for JM

I

In 1834, when Alexander Kinglake
stood by the banks of the Sava River,
at the frontier of the Ottoman Empire,
and bid farewell to his friends, he turned
and saw the border officer stride toward him
with his hand outstretched, asking once more
if he was ready to leave the civilized world.

He knew this man had been exposed to the plague,
that he lived in "a state of perpetual
excommunication" under the yellow flag
that hung above the quarantine station.
In that moment Kinglake paused to consider
how he was about to cross the boundary
between Christendom and the Orient,
between the righteous and ungodly, cleanliness
and disease, even between the living
and the dead. He saw great vultures wheeling
over the city on the other side:
this was Belgrade, but might as well have been
the port-of-entry to the underworld.
He saw the oarsmen waiting in the boat
and thought of the ferry across the River Styx
and of Charon, who was now approaching him
in the guise of the Austrian border officer.

He had prepared himself for his departure
"with nearly as much solemnity" as someone
"departing this life," but now he felt
the sudden joy of being free at last
of "the stale civilization of Europe,"
of the "state of utter respectability"

which had imprisoned him in England.
He thrilled at the thought of being robbed
or murdered by fierce-eyed men in turbans.
He did not recoil from the border officer's
outstretched hand, but met it with his own
and gripped it firmly, ready to embrace
"the Splendour and Havoc of The East."

II

Despite its dandified bravado, that handshake
marked a firm resolve, some might even say
an obsession. For his entire journey
Kinglake took no precautions against the plague,
as if the absolute freedom he craved
included the possibility of death.
He spurned the other Europeans he saw
weaving through the streets of Constantinople
trying not to be touched, "slinking from death,"
and in contempt for them and all that they stood for
he touched the lolling foot of a plague-stricken corpse
that passed by in a funeral procession.

The presence of the plague was a stimulant
he came to need, bracing his nerves
with an "unusual animation"
and lending him the proper "reverence and awe"
to regard the remnants of dead empires.
In Cairo, where the plague was in full force,
he woke each morning to the howls of mourners
who trailed the biers that passed incessantly
below his window, and he savored the air
"thick with the fragrance of burial spice."

Two Salutations

Like the Moslems, Kinglake put his faith
in Destiny, and walked serenely through the streets.
He came to believe that those who lived in fear,
constantly checking for symptoms of the plague –
the parched mouth, throbbing brain, and rapid pulse,
the lump like a bullet lodged under the arm –
these people brought the symptoms on themselves
and soon became the food of squalling jackals:
like the moneychanger who hoarded his days like coins
and snatched the bills from Kinglake's hand with tongs
but not long afterward died of the plague.

How different was the noble old Osmanli
who was his host in the village of Sakkara,
which the plague had left alone. Even so,
this man at first did not touch his guest
out of deference to European fears.
But as soon as it was clear that he, not Kinglake,
would be the person endangered by contact,
he gently laid his hand on Kinglake's arm
and welcomed him as one who had been blessed.

Desert Knowledge

We rode all day on camels and at night
slept under the stars, but it dawned on us
that every turn our camel drivers made
around the massive dunes was calculated
to avoid another group like ours.
They were experts, and we never saw the others.
Still, it came as something of a letdown
to learn that these same dunes had been used
as a backdrop in hundreds of Hindi movies.
How far from civilization could we be?
Not for us the exultation of leaving it
all behind that Alexander Kinglake felt
a hundred and sixty years before, riding
for days across the desert without seeing
anyone outside of his small caravan.
Not for us the thrill that shot through him
when he saw a speck on the shimmering horizon
moving toward him. Who would it be? –
a Bedouin who would rob him? Slowly
the speck became two specks, then two camels
with two riders, then something truly strange:
an English gentleman in a shooting jacket
and his servant, slouching along beside him.
As they approached, Kinglake kept turning over
the question of whether or not to speak
and decided against it, not wanting to give up
the silence and broad solitude of the desert.
The other must have made the same decision,
because the two Englishmen passed each other
just as they would have on a busy street
in London, tipping their caps without a word –
a gesture which, in the desert's isolation,
seemed absurd and left an aftertaste
of disappointment, as if they'd seen themselves
reflected in the mirror of the desert.

As for us, crossing and recrossing our stage set,
even this bitter knowledge was denied us.

Lord, Deliver Us from This Affliction

It starts when you say the grapevines, splayed
on wires, look like twisted crucifixes,
and that the hillside vineyards we wind past
in our little rented Fiat
are graveyards of the chosen.
And now that Easter has arrived,
so has the resurrection of the vines:
a few green leaves and shoots uncurl
which, later on, will yield the blood of Christ.

Our windshield frames a fresco
brought to life, and where the road
bends, two cherry trees in white sleeves
perform a pantomime Annunciation.
The landscape itself is spired
with cypresses, and the new green wheat
spreads rich and flowing vestments on the fields.
By evening, a monastery on a hill,
its bricks infused with pink light, seems

almost a miracle: a place to stay.
But it's just chance, and we're just passing through.
The crucifix between the beds
separates us only for one night,
and we'd be happy if the rain
that's just begun to drum the tile roof
washed clean our sleeping minds
so that tomorrow we can see
the world afresh, for what it truly is.

Letter from the Golden Triangle

Just beyond the porch of our bamboo bungalow
a muddy river quietly flows by,
and on the other side, which is Burma,
brown-skinned children splash one another
and Buddhist monks in saffron robes
sit in the shade- and sun-splotched groves,
meditating alone or talking in groups
as the day slowly comes to a close.

We've spent the last few days scouring
the countryside on a rented Honda *Dream*,
looking for poppy fields – rumor has it
they're in bloom now, but nobody knows where,
and it's not exactly the right question to ask.
So far they exist only in our minds,
like a dream induced by the very opium
they'll yield. They're the missing pieces

of an endless jigsaw puzzle of rice fields,
yellow and shorn, harvest long over.
We saw it from above when we rode up a mountain
past waterfalls and lush cascades of vegetation,
the great green plumage of banana trees,
red and white poinsettia growing wild,
palm trees, of course, and all sorts of flowers
we can't identify (but no poppies).

On top stood a temple with a garish red roof
and an enormous stupa plated with gold,
like a bell ringing silently against the blue.
There was a Buddha covered and fluttering
with gold leaf applied by worshipers,
and more of those shaven-headed monks.
Miles below, the Mekong, like a thick
brown snake, slid along the border of Laos.

Letter from the Golden Triangle

We've come to the end of our last afternoon.
We never found the poppies or smoked opium,
but our leaving tomorrow colors the moment
with the mild opiate of anticipated nostalgia,
making the light grow yellower, as the absence
of the motorcycle's blare, which filled
our ears all day, opens up the silence.
Sunlight and silence have become

one substance, as if that gold bell on the mountain
were ringing its silence through the whole valley,
turning everything to gold: the rice fields, the river,
the skin of swimming children, the bamboo houses –
and now a butterfly the color of the monks' robes
(as if one of them had just been transfigured)
flutters across the river, catching the light
like a piece of gold leaf in the breeze.

Political Poem

Gone are the days,
are the centuries, even,
when government officials
retired to become
poets in gardens
of their own design,
as here in Suzhou
happened for so long:
a gnarled shaft
of limestone here,
there a willow's
green locks swaying
above the fishpond,
a zigzag bridge
to a pagoda where,
far from the capital,
one could finally
attend to matters
of real importance:
the moon's reflection
troubled by a carp.

Sketch

for Donald Richie

August 1945. The bombs
had fallen, the war was coming to an end.
By a deserted canal outside Shanghai,
a young American merchant marine ensign
sat sketching a pagoda. A rhythmic clanking,
rising behind the cicadas' shimmering scrim,
broke through to consciousness too late: he looked up
and saw a platoon of Japanese soldiers
marching toward him along the canal path.
Fear bolted through him, but he made himself
keep sketching as the soldiers filed past
behind him, his heart fisting when he saw,
out of the corner of his eye, the rear officer
veer toward him as the troops continued on.
He heard the crunch of boots against loose stones
halting at his back. The pencil stopped.
The sketchbook on his knee seemed far away,
as if seen through the wrong end of a telescope.
Then the page went blank and he saw nothing
except an image of the officer's raised sword
scything down on him, and of his head
splashing into the canal's stagnant water.
The officer barked something in Japanese,
a phrase that bored itself into the brain
of the young American, who took it to be
the formal pronouncement of his execution.
But the sword never fell, and the American
told me his story forty-three years later
while we were having lunch at the Press Club
on the top floor of a Tokyo high-rise
with a view of the Imperial Palace.
Emperor Hirohito was dying,
and hundreds of people were standing in the rain
before the palace gates, waiting in line

to sign their last respects into a book.
From that height, their umbrellas seemed to form
the scales of a long, sinuous dragon.
"Which, after all, is an imperial symbol,"
said my host. But his story wasn't finished.
Not long after the war, he'd come to Japan
and found he loved the place. He never left.
Years later, after he'd learned Japanese,
the utterance from that day emerged intact,
like a dormant insect larva that had lodged
in his skull and was now coming back to life
as something wholly different: not a sentence
of death, but the phrase *Nakanaka yoi*,
meaning, in reference to the sketch, "Not bad at all."

A Shave by the Ganges

Sleepwalking from one ghat to the next,
I came to the place where the barbers
all hunkered down, their bony knees akimbo,
dhotis bunched around their loins like diapers,
the tools of their trade laid out on burlap mats:
straight razors, scissors, combs, battered brass bowls.

Not once in my life had I been shaved by a barber,
but I sat down then to wait my turn.
I'd come this far, I'd just seen a foot
twisting up like a flag from a cremation,
I wanted to be shaved in that holy city
as if I were part of a daily ritual.

So I was happy to pay my two rupees
and surrender my face to those dark skilled hands
that slapped the foam on with a shaving brush
and worked the razor quickly across my cheek.
Sitting there as he turned my head this way
and that, I saw the crowds of bathers

in the river below, the temple stupas
looming overhead, as if about to fall,
a skeletal umbrella, a legless beggar
lolling on a dolly – all at angles odd enough
to make me see them finally, and feel
the razor's edge against my throat.

Double Exposure

My great-grandfather's photo albums
from his trip around the world in 1905,
their suede covers printed with his name
in gold capitals, and their brittle pages
torn loose and out of order, show him
in the Philippines with William Howard Taft
(round as the world, big as an elephant),
then *on* an elephant in India,
wearing a pith helmet and staring out
from behind his black, indelible moustache
as if he owned the world ...
                    a world
I can't recognize (Hong Kong's bristling
crystallization of skyscrapers
dissolved to a sediment of shacks),
and a man I never knew, with whom
I feel no bond beyond the facts
of my middle name and an inheritance
of genes by now reshuffled as
these pages I turn.
                  But wait! Here's one
of Varanasi, just as I saw it
a year ago – and all at once I'm looking
with his eyes through the viewfinder
of his camera with the black bellows extended,
then letting it fall and feeling its weight
against the back of the neck as the scene
just caught on film – a body in flames
crumpling as the pyre underneath it
collapses – burns itself into the brain
which can't contain it, can't stop the fire
from spreading through all the internal organs
and into the limbs, until the knees give way
and he has to sit down.
                  He sits there

Double Exposure

for a long time, dazed, not sure what has happened,
then gets up and leaves me on the stone steps
in the exact spot he rose from, while he
wanders off along the ghats, ghost-like,
in the shadows of temples piled like stalagmites,
to join the multitude of spectral figures
who have traveled here for centuries,
disappearing behind a hazy veil
of smoke rising from the funeral pyres
and the emulsion's silvery sheen.

Gift

for James Merrill, in memory

This helix of wheat
has hung by a thread
from the windowframe
for years now,
almost weightless,
spinning sometimes
when a breeze
comes through the screen.
A token of fertility,
you brought it back
from the Peloponnese
and passed it on to me
because, seeing it
among the oddments
on your mantelpiece,
I marveled at
its ingenuity –
also, I think, because
it answered my wish
for a child. The sun,
some mornings, plays
on your gift, turning it
into a spiral cage
of light; other times
it hangs in shadow
and takes on the weight
of your death –
and yet the thread
still holds. These months
I've felt the pull
of this wheatstalk whorl
again and again
and, thinking of you,
looked up to see it

Gift

suspended there
between two worlds,
in the changing light.

Swifts at Evening

The whoosh of rush hour traffic washes through my head
as I cross the bridge through the treetops into my neighborhood
and what's left of my thoughts is sucked up suddenly
by a huge whirlwind of birds, thousands of chimney swifts
wheeling crazily overhead against a sky just beginning
to deepen into evening – turning round and round
in their erratic spiral ragged at the edges
where more chittering birds join in the circling
flock from every direction, having spent all
day on the wing scattered for miles across
September skies and now pulled into the
great vortex that funnels into the air-
shaft of the library, the whole day
going like water down a drain with
the sucking sound of traffic and
the birds swirling like specks
of living sediment drawn from
the world into the whirlpool
into the word-pool flapping
like bats at the last
moment diving and
turning into
words.

The Birds That Woke Us: An Urban Pastoral

It wasn't the rooster's familiar cry
piercing the air, but often the wonk
of something stranger (a crane?), and the mind,
still half in dream, watched the jungle's steam
lift, revealing oak and beech – and remembered
the zoo concealed behind that mass of green.
We lived in a tree house, or a tree
apartment. We could lie in bed and watch
a dove perched on the windowsill, calling us
out of sleep with a low moan, its opal head
pulled in and breast puffed plushly out – or catch
a glimpse of the pileated woodpecker
ratcheting around tree trunks and rattling
as it flew off, as if to set the woods
on fire with the flame of its red crest.
Were they some kind of sign? We took them
for luck, and now that our arboreal life
has ended, they have become emblems
of that green and buoyant era. We'd learned
to sleep right through the muffled wail of sirens
spiraling up from another part of town,
to keep at a safe distance whatever
emergencies they signified. The wren
was our alarm clock on most days,
its bright dactyls ringing through the trees:
"Tea kettle, tea kettle, tea kettle, tea kettle, tea."
We'd get up and, yes, put on the tea kettle.
They seemed to parallel our life in these
small ways, and flavor it: like the cardinal
that sometimes sang to us at breakfast
from a branch not six feet from the window,
notes dripping sweetly from its stout bill
like syrup through the spout of a pitcher
or drops of honey splashing in our tea.

The Speckled Egg

On the first day you felt well enough,
we walked to the cathedral (not to pray,
though merely walking there is a form of prayer),
past houses that we'd often let ourselves
dream of living in some day, lovely houses
on whose front porches children played.

My eyes fell to the herringbone brick walk
heaved up by the dark roots
of giant sycamores that lined the street.
There I found a small bird's egg, speckled brown.
We looked up: the white arms of the sycamore
had let it fall during the storm.

I knew we must be thinking the same thing.
The world had handed us a metaphor
that was cold comfort now, after our loss.
Too perfect, despite the hairline crack
from which the yolk had leaked and dried,
too weightless for what it signified.

But I couldn't let it go, I kept the egg,
rolling it over and over in my palm,
wanting to believe such happenstance
was telling me the world made sense
and had its reasons
for what it gave and what it took away.

I washed the yolk off in the garden's fountain,
and we sampled basil, sage, and thyme,
then sat on a bench. We didn't go inside.
And I didn't say what I was thinking then
because I didn't want to make you cry:
that the crane reaching over the bell tower

The Speckled Egg

(waiting to lower the last stone into place)
was part of a deus ex machina
that would not happen, the god swooping down
on cue to take the egg from my hand
then soaring up to place it carefully
in the nest, the crack miraculously
sealed again, the embryo alive.

Foreshadowing

Two days before I left for Mexico
to see the eclipse, we watched a litmus strip
turn blue, and knew you were pregnant. Sunlight
brightened the apartment all morning,
then slipped away as thunderheads built up
and darkened with a superstitious fear:
that the eclipse would be an omen for another
miscarriage, a blighted ovum in the sky.
I kept this thought from you, shutting it inside me
as tightly as the locals shut themselves
inside their houses on the day of the eclipse.
They too were superstitious, having knotted
scarlet rags to their gateposts. My friends and I
ignored those warnings, climbed a barren hill
that overlooked the Pacific, and waited.
Slowly the noon light grew lunar, penumbral,
and the landscape turned to silver. The ocean
was a pewter foil, moving in calm swells
below a saffron glow on the horizon.
Above, a few stars glimmered into being.
A tinge of ancient fear rippled through me,
and I shivered as the temperature dropped
and time went backwards: huge granite outcrops
reared like dinosaurs, three frigate birds
sailed overhead, as big as pterodactyls.
The shadow swept across the face of the water,
and I looked up and saw the sun implode
into a single spark that flickered out
as a black disk slid into place
like a lid, and the corona spread
in great feathery plumes of luminous gas,
the unseen made visible, and given
the power of vision: a single eye
stared down from the top of the sky –
the perfect black pupil, solar flares

like backlit blood vessels, and the corona's
diaphanous iris opening. An eye
with wings of light, ethereal, seraphic,
hovering at the zenith and looking down
to where I floated in a stratosphere
of wonder like the one from which, months later,
I looked down to watch the crowning head
emerge, the plates of the skull bulging
under the wet black hair, the purple face
staring up with wide unblinking eyes.

Arrival

After Christopher Smart

I will consider my son William,

who came into the world two weeks early, as if he couldn't wait;

who was carried on a river that gushed from his mother;

who was purple with matted black hair;

who announced his arrival not by crying but by peeing, with the
umbilical cord still attached;

who looked all around with wide slate-blue eyes and smacked his
lips as if to taste the world;

who took to his mother's breast right away;

who sucks my little finger with such vigor that it feels as if he's
going to pull my fingernail right off;

who sometimes refuses my finger, screwing up his face in disgust
as if I have stuck a pickled radish into his mouth;

whose face is beautiful and not like a shriveled prune;

whose hair, though black, is soft as milkweed;

who was born with long eyelashes that girls will someday envy;

whose fingernails are minuscule, thin and pliable;

whose toes are like caterpillars;

whose penis is a little acorn;

whose excrement is like the finest mustard;

who can squeak like a mouse and bleat like a lamb;

who hiccups and his whole body convulses;

who screams and turns red and kicks sometimes when we change
his diaper;

who when he stops screaming is probably peeing;

whose deep sobs from the back of his throat bring tears to my own
eyes;

who likes to be carried in a pouched sling;

who thinks he is a marsupial;

who has soft fur on his shoulders, back, and legs;

who is nocturnal and whose eyes are widest at night;

who will sleep sometimes if I lay him across my chest;

whose eyes flutter, whose nostrils dilate, and whose mouth
twitches into strange grimaces and smiles as he dreams;

who is full of the living spirit which causes his body to wiggle and
   squirm;
who stretches his arms and arches his back and you can feel his
   great strength;
who lies with the soles of his feet together, as if praying with his
   feet;
who is a blessing upon our household and upon the world;
who doesn't know where the world ends and he begins;
who is himself the world;
who has a sweet smell.

The Place

After years of going back to a place you love,
you may have so many memories of the place
that whenever you think about it you become
calm and still as the lake at evening
when the hills and trees are mirrored there.
You can imagine your way back any time,
following trails you know by heart, with arteries
of roots, and you hold onto the place inside
the way the tentacled roots of a birch
grip a granite boulder shagged with ferns.
But there is always something calling you back
further, to childhood summers spent there,
or even further, beyond specific memories,
until memory itself, in its purest form,
is made of blue lakes nestled into foothills
and rivers the color of ale plunging over
rust-orange rocks then deepening for long still stretches
where pines and hemlocks lean out over the bank,
as you lean too, thinking, wherever you are.
And when you think of actually going back,
you can already feel how that place in you
will go rushing out to meet the real place,
which, itself, will lie before you, more vivid
than you remembered it, or more vivid because
you remembered it, each layer of your memory
adding a bluer gloss to the lake's surface
and polishing the leaves until they shine.

from Feeding the Fire (2001)

Green Canoe

I don't often get the chance any longer
to go out alone in the green canoe
and, lying in the bottom of the boat,
just drift where the breeze takes me,
down to the other end of the lake
or into some cove without my knowing
because I can't see anything over
the gunwales but sky as I lie there,
feeling the ribs of the boat as my own,
this floating pod with a body inside it ...

also a mind, that drifts among clouds
and the sounds that carry over water –
a flutter of birdsong, a screen door
slamming shut – as well as the usual stuff
that clutters it, but slowed down, opened up,
like the fluff of milkweed tugged
from its husk and floating over the lake,
to be mistaken for mayflies at dusk
by feeding trout, or be carried away
to a place where the seeds might sprout.

Lure

"What a sexy name for a piece of fishing gear,"
said Mrs Stevens. At nine or ten
I wasn't old enough to know what she meant.
I was casting a Phoebe Wobbler or a Daredevil
off the end of the dock, and I wasn't
getting any strikes. Blonde hair pulled back,
a few wisps of it falling across her forehead,
high cheekbones, long suntanned legs
beneath her short tennis skirt – these were things
I didn't pay much attention to back then
and remember dimly, as if they were underwater.
She was probably ten years younger
than I am now. I couldn't understand
why she was making such a big deal
about a word. I just kept casting
and reeling in the clear line, pushing and releasing
the button on my Zebco. I didn't even have to pretend
I didn't catch on, and it never got weird
being alone with her down there on the dock.
The waters of adulthood were unfathomable,
though I sensed in the clinking drinks
and cocktail laughter of my parents and their friends
something silvery flashing under the surface.
Mrs Stevens could have been up to anything
or nothing. Maybe she was just practicing
her grown-up talk, or maybe she was flirting,
testing me. Maybe she already knew
she was going to leave her husband in a few years,
listing among her reasons that he wasn't good enough
at tennis. He already had the sad eyes
of a dog who'd been abandoned by the highway.
I saw him ten years later, when I was in college,
sitting alone in one of those bars with lobster traps
and trophy fish on the walls, fishing nets
draped from the ceiling. After our surprised hellos,

Lure

neither of us found much to say, and as I stood there
trying not to look into his bereft face,
I thought of how sexy his ex-wife used to be
and what it was like to be a kid
intent on hooking brook trout or rainbows.

Our Other Sister

for Ellen

The cruelest thing I did to my younger sister
wasn't shooting a homemade blowdart into her knee,
where it dangled for a breathless second

before dropping off, but telling her we had
another, older sister who'd gone away.
What my motives were I can't recall: a whim,

or was it some need of mine to toy with loss,
to probe the ache of imaginary wounds?
But that first sentence was like a strand of DNA

that replicated itself in coiling lies
when my sister began asking her desperate questions.
I called our older sister Isabel

and gave her hazel eyes and long blonde hair.
I had her run away to California
where she took drugs and made hippie jewelry.

Before I knew it, she'd moved to Santa Fe
and opened a shop. She sent a postcard
every year or so, but she'd stopped calling.

I can still see my younger sister staring at me,
her eyes widening with desolation
then filling with tears. I can still remember

how thrilled and horrified I was
that something I'd just made up
had that kind of power, and I can still feel

the blowdart of remorse stabbing me in the heart
as I rushed to tell her none of it was true.
But it was too late. Our other sister

had already taken shape, and we could not
call her back from her life far away
or tell her how badly we missed her.

Family Dog

A succession of Newfoundlands
of diminishing nobility
and with names like English maids –
Flossie, Rosie, Nelly –
gave way, long after I'd left,
to this hyperactive black lab
who (like me?) never grew up,
always the exuberant puppy
to almost everyone's annoyance,
and whose name – Jess – is so much
like my own that when I'm home
and hear my father call the dog
or say his name in irritation
when he's gotten in the garbage
or chewed up someone's shoe,
I'm forced to relive an unpleasant
split second I lived many times
as a teenager, when my father
and I were chronic enemies –
a quick shock through my heart
and the thought, *Oh God, what
have I done now?* Followed now
by the realization, *It's only the dog,*
a sigh of relief, a quiet laugh ...
I'm almost always fooled,
as if the pitch of my father's voice
triggered some switch
in my nervous system, my body
still wired for sound
decades later, bringing back,
before I have time to think,
the fear, the rancor,
things I would rather forget,
the way a dog forgets
and always comes back, comes home

Family Dog

when his name is called,
knowing his master loves him.

My Double Nonconversion

(NYC, 1976)

I must have been looking up at the stars
on the vaulted ceiling, that simulacrum of heaven,
as the muffled bustle of arrivals and departures
washed over me like surf. I must have looked
so young and unstreetwise in my wonder,
standing like that in Grand Central's concourse,
a perfect target for the skinhead in saffron robe
who greeted me and pushed into my hands
a garish edition of the *Bhagavad-Gita*.
And I must have been a very different person
from the one I later became, to stay
and talk with him, and even buy the book.

I'm trying to remember what it felt like
to be that person, a novitiate to the city
open to any approach. Less than a minute
after leaving the Hare Krishna, still inside
the basilical concourse, I allowed myself
to be waylaid by a young man with a Bible,
listened to the passages he quoted,
then (this is the part I can hardly believe)
knelt down with him in a bank of phone booths
and prayed, delirious with self-consciousness
as if God Himself were watching. Afterward,
he said a seed had been planted inside me.

That copy of the *Bhagavad-Gita* has slipped
into the gulf of twenty years between then and now,
and that seed has gone untended just as long.
When I left the Born-Again, I took the subway
uptown to Columbia, where I was a freshman,
then the dingy elevator up to my monklike cell:
one bed, one desk, one chair, one dresser, one window
facing a roofscape to the south, and open sky.

My Double Nonconversion

Also, a fern I'd bought my first day there
in front of St John the Divine, from an old woman
who told me, with a look of crazed belief,
that someday it would grow into a tree.

Time Smear

Julie's driving, I'm in the passenger seat
wearing holographic glasses that give the world
a prismatic aura as it all speeds by,
the Grateful Dead are playing on the stereo
for the first time in ages, and I feel
those ages rushing through me in reverse
until it's summer eighteen years ago.
We're on our way out to Colorado
to look for jobs, my brother Jeremy
in the back seat making peanut butter
and jelly sandwiches for lunch. We're just kids
though we don't think of it that way,
and the jobs we find will be just the kind of jolt
to our uncompleted college educations
we're looking for: Jeremy and I digging ditches
and planting trees in a soon-to-be-yet-another
golf course community, and Julie scooping
ice cream in Vail, a town so artificial
it's like a confection itself, a mall display
or children's board game surrounded by mountains.
Our boss, who lives there, is a smooth preener-type
we refer to as "Chip Ramsey, male prostitute."
I'm writing poems but would never dream
of putting him in one of them, or for that matter
the mobile home we've rented by the highway
where, at the end of the day, we drink beer and sit
really low on the couch so the bottom edge
of the picture window cuts the other trailers
out of the view and we just see mountains.
We're masquerading as the working class
and not quite pulling it off, knowing we'll be
out of there in a matter of weeks, but it feels good
to have jobs we can complain about and which,
for all three of us in fact, strengthen our arms.
But this is all a week or so away, we're still

driving out there, taking turns behind the wheel
of a French's-Mustard-colored AMC Hornet,
a truly crappy car that can barely catch its breath
on any kind of incline at higher altitudes.
Last night we slept on the bank of a river
wrapped in the thick cocoon of the rapids' roar,
and this morning we had rainbows for breakfast,
early sunlight haloing the leaping spray.
We don't need much, just the adrenaline
of driving is enough, the jittery hum
of sleeplessness in our veins, the slipping back
and forth between reflection and ecstasy
the Dead keep making happen, giving me
goose bumps now as they make their way between
"Not Fade Away" and "Going Down the Road
Feeling Bad," though I'm not feeling bad at all,
I'm feeling quite good, because it's the transitions
I've always loved, that sense of being
two places at once and in neither one,
the music taking me all the way out and back
to this car with Julie driving and behind us
our son and daughter sitting in the back seat
laughing at me rocking to the music, saying
"Daddy, can we have our silly glasses back?"

Salt

I'm not sure when it started,
    the family tradition
        of using kosher salt,

coarse grains pinched
        between forefinger and thumb
            then held above our plates

and sprinkled down like snow
        on meat, potatoes, carrots.
            I didn't even know

what kosher meant
        until I was older,
            the six-pointed star

on the package was not yet
        a symbol of any kind,
            only a star of special interest

because it was made
        ingeniously of two
            triangles superimposed.

I had never eaten
        or even heard of bagels
            until I got to college,

where my neighbors
        in the dorm had names
            like Immerman, Perlstein,

Adelman, and Platnik.
        They had mezuzahs
            on their doorframes

Salt

like strange doorbells.
  Michael Chuback,
    a few doors down the hall,

had a pennant on his wall
  emblazoned with the words
    YESHIVA OF FLATBUSH,

a phrase so alien to me
  it might have been the name
    of a Hindu deity.

They teased me
  for being a WASP,
    but also took me in,

took me to their homes
  in Queens or New Jersey,
    where their parents

said things like, "I can't
  believe it: a goy in my house,"
    and told me stories

of how *their* parents
  escaped the Gestapo
    or didn't, of growing up

on the Lower East Side,
  whole families in one room,
    stories that left me

speechless, feeling as if
  I had no history
    to speak of.

Salt

And then I fell in love
　　　with you, the heir
　　　　　of Lithuanian Jews,

drawn first by the beauty
　　　of your eyes –
　　　　　mildly exotic

yet instantly familiar,
　　　suggesting a world
　　　　　unknown to me

but which I longed
　　　to return to. And there
　　　　　I have remained, through all

the changes in our lives,
　　　the history we've
　　　　　created together.

Now, in a new house again,
　　　I sprinkle kosher salt
　　　　　in the corners of the rooms

as a Jewish friend of ours
　　　instructed me to do –
　　　　　an old tradition

to ward off evil spirits –
　　　the salt of my childhood
　　　　　and that of your ancestry

mingling in this
　　　partly ridiculous
　　　　　partly sacred act.

Rowing

How many years have we been doing this together,
me in the bow rowing, you in the stern
lying back, dragging your hands in the water –
or, as now, the other way around, your body
moving toward me and away, your dark hair swinging
forward and back, your face flushed and lovely
against the green hills, the blues of lake and sky.

Soon nothing else matters but this pleasure,
your green eyes looking past me, far away,
then at me, then away, your lips I want to kiss
each time they come near me, your arms that reach
toward me gripping the handles as the blades
swing back dripping, two arcs of droplets
pearling on the surface before disappearing.

Sometimes I think we could do this forever,
like part of the vow we share, the rhythm
we find, the pull of each stroke on the muscles
of your arched back, your neck gorged and pulsing
with the work of it, your body rocking
more urgently now, your face straining with something
like pain you can hardly stand – then letting go,

the two of us gliding out over the water.

The Burning Hat

Whatever grief my parents felt
was lost on me, or is lost to me now.
But I do remember the Panama hat
that they brought back from the apartment
of Whoever-It-Was (a great-great-aunt?)
and gave to me. All afternoon I wore it
(despite the way it fell over my eyes),
pretending I was in a far-off country
where the hat brim fended off the sun
that blazed all day, even in winter.
I finally took it off at dinnertime,
placing it beside me on the bench
where I sat with my back to the fire.
The next thing I remember is how it fell
into the fireplace, and how it felt
to see it blaze up with the sound
of a great wind: unbearable. I reached
for the flames, then, through a blur of tears,
saw something amazing: the hat began to shrink –
smaller and smaller, yet holding its shape,
until I thought it was going to disappear
and screamed for it to stop. It stopped.
And there it was, more precious than before,
a perfect hat for a doll or puppet – too small for me
but longed for all the more. The flames
had died; a few small sparks crawled over it
with icy tinkling sounds. I held my breath,
then let it out again in a mournful sob
when that ghostly hat broke into ashes.

Vietnam Scrapbook

Midway through fourth grade, early 1968,
Mrs Hackemeyer said it was time
we learned about the war in Vietnam,
where, she said, "American boys
are giving their lives to fight communism."
We were American boys, or half of us were,
and we already knew communism was bad,
how it spread like a rash across the map
that pulled down like an illustrated window shade.

The paper maps that Mrs Hackemeyer passed out
were scented with her perfume and showed a country
shaped vaguely like a seahorse, its slender waist
adorned with a slim, candy-striped belt
we labeled *DMZ*. We added stars and dots
and printed in *Saigon, Hanoi, Khe Sanh,
the Gulf of Tonkin, the Mekong River, Hue* –
names so strange they seemed to come
from an Asian version of *The Hobbit*,

which the librarian was reading aloud to us
in daily installments. Ho Chi Minh
might have been the leader of the evil goblins.
It was another world with its own vocabulary words –
"Charlie," chopper, napalm, punji –
words we lobbed like make-believe hand grenades
during recess, among our screams
of phony agony, our diving death-sprawls.
POWs were thrown into the jungle gym.

But they all escaped as soon as the bell rang,
the dead sprang up and ran inside
where Mrs Hackemeyer tried to teach us
"the horror of war." *Horror* meant Godzilla,
and *Viet Cong* reminded us of King Kong.

Horror made you munch your popcorn faster.
Even after we started pasting photographs
from *Time* and *Life* into our notebooks – a task
that lasted weeks – it never broke through.

We clipped the jungle's blooming fireballs
with safety scissors, smeared minty paste
on the screaming napalm-victim's back,
pressed the blood- and mud-spattered soldiers
into clean white pages, a little ink
smudging off on our soft, sticky fingertips,
as Mrs Hackemeyer leaned over us
in her thick, invisible cloud of perfume,
smoke from bombed cities rising up in black plumes.

Golden Retriever

... bounding again into those childhood fields
with the dumb trust that nothing found in them
can hurt you. How long can this willed
innocence go on? Endlessly, it seems,
as long as you can make yourself believe
the world loves you. It's an old trick:
no matter how many times the stick
is thrown into the past, those days come back
drenched in the slobber of nostalgia.
Some dogs will go on fetching like that
until they literally drop dead
from exhaustion, faithful to the end —
but not to the way things really happened.
It's all the result of selective
memory, sniffing out the Golden Moments
while ignoring the carpet's yellow stains,
emblems (don't you remember?) of the shame
you were made to feel when your snout was thrust
in the puddle of urine or pile of shit
and a hand beat you. Shouldn't those primal scenes
be replayed, too? Forget the fucking stick.
Go find something really putrid to roll in
and smear all over your golden fur. Go on.

The Diver

We hawked and spat into our masks, slipped on our flippers,
gripped the rubber mouthpiece of the snorkel in our teeth,
and swam out, peering into the lake's green interior,
each enclosed in the cocoon of his own breathing ...
and in our different lives: he was a local
with a hick accent I mimicked behind his back,
I one of the privileged summer residents
he resented. Yet we were friends, bound together
by our seasonal crush on the same girl
and this almost daily ritual, the allure
of what mysterious treasures we might discover:
mostly old bottles, tossed off docks and boathouses
three generations back. Beer, whiskey, gin
and medicine bottles, seamless bottles of spun glass,
and old round-bottomed soda water bottles
of aquamarine glass, thick and full of bubbles,
like objects formed from the lake's own water
under the pressure and icy temperature
of depths we could hardly reach in one breath.

We used to scare ourselves with talk about "the bends"
and nitrogen narcosis, names which, with their tang
of death, we loved to say, though we were in no danger
kicking down through the thermocline, ears squeaking
on the eerie frequency of that submarine twilight
as we reached into the bottom's murk in search of something
worth bringing to light. Later, it became his life:
frogman in the army, then in a diving business.
He was behind the wheel of his pickup when the embolism
hit his brain – no chance for him to take a breath
before going under that last time, and yet the depth
was too much to fathom when I imagined him
down there, as in the old days: always outlasting me,
his skin glowing faintly with an unreal whiteness
when I took one final look at him in the dim light

The Diver

before rushing up in a cloud of mushrooming bubbles
toward the mirrory underside of the surface,
legs furiously pumping as my lungs collapsed –
then plunging into daylight with a violent gasp.

The Oval Pin

sits on your dresser,
a gift a friend brought back from Russia:
a troika painted on black lacquer.

The three horses, one plunging forward,
one rearing up, one looking back
at the man and woman in the sleigh,

have some traditional significance
(she must have told you the story)
that you no longer remember.

You sense some urgency
in the way the man raises his whip
high, like the slimmest gold banner,

in the anxious expression
the artist managed to portray
on the woman's minuscule face,

and in the blanket or shawl
that trails and flaps behind the sleigh
like a twisted cloud of green smoke –

or almost like a shrouded body.
Something is wrong. A friend is ill
and dying. They must hurry.

But though the horses gallop wildly
like mythical beasts, with coats
of orange and pink and manes of flame,

though the sleigh lifts up and flies
through the night as black as lacquer,
these two on their dire errand

The Oval Pin

will never arrive in time to see
their friend alive, to say good-bye –
as we will never see again

the friend who gave you
this oval pin, which you reach for now
and fasten to your black dress.

(Ann Rubin, 1962-1998)

White Spaces

(Bert M-P. Leefmans, 1918-1980)

... hovering at the edges, elusive, he inhabits
spaces I would rather not clutter with words.

Even so, your words brought him back to me
and helped me find my own, remembering
that first day, when he lectured on Baudelaire
to five of us and a lot of empty seats,
speaking methodically, head in a cloud
of cigarette smoke, his frail hunched body
shuffling back and forth through a dust of ash.

He was not a romantic figure. More like
cut glass, chiseled, thin, emaciated, bent.

Soon we were meeting in his apartment
on Morningside, that street whose curving sweep
led us back to the turn of the century.
We pored over poems by Mallarmé,
surrounded by dozing snakes in glass cases
(he kept the mice to feed them in the kitchen).
He had a languid quality, like those snakes

– and something underneath, something like
the tautness of wire cutting down to truth –

working his way slowly through a poem
with a submerged urgency, examining
each word, while keeping all of them in view,
intent on any signalings between them.
"What matters is the relationship between
the words," he'd say, "and the spaces around them."
They wavered and swerved under our gaze,

White Spaces

... shrugging and moving away, always on the move –
he wouldn't or couldn't stay with his persona.

but as he spoke their oscillation slowed,
until the whole poem seemed to crystallize,
to hover free and luminous above the page.
But poetry was also bound to life
by words – he wanted us to see that, too –
a notion out of fashion among his colleagues,
who treated him as though his time had passed.

He knew about power and didn't want it.
He tore up almost everything he wrote.

I can almost hear him saying it's hopeless,
this effort to put him into words – both mine
and yours, who wish to go unnamed.
Your letter about him put me to shame.
You who knew him so much better than I did
saw the futility, though you went on
for three typed pages at the speed of passion:

He knew about beauty but wasn't possessive about it.
He knew about letting go of what he wanted.

One day when I revealed to him my dream
of writing "a whole new kind of poetry,"
he scolded me for "taking the wrong approach.
Just write the poems that come naturally.
Whether or not they're new is unimportant.
They have to come from you. Remember that."
I did, years later, but not in time to thank him.

... knowledge carried lightly, that nonchalance he kept
to the very end, when his heart was failing him.

White Spaces

I was too young and busy with my own life
even to notice he was sick, to be alarmed
by the cough that came from deep within his chest.
But one day my last semester, entering campus,
I saw the university's pale blue flag
at half-mast and instinctively changed course –
past Rodin's sullen *Thinker*, green with age,

An unconvinced survivor of his own life.
Le prince d'Aquitaine à la tour abolie.

into Philosophy, and up to his office door,
where a note explained he'd died the night before ...
Gone now, known too briefly and too long ago
for me to bring him back in a poem,
though I'd like to think that what he was
and what he gave me hover at the edges
of these lines, in the white spaces around them

... always asking what can be found in words
and what forever lies beyond them.

Medusa

(The New England Aquarium)

Like fireworks, but alive,
a nebula exploding
over and over in a liquid sky,
this undulant soft bell
of jellyfish glowing orange
and trailing a baroque
mane of streamers, so
exquisite in its fluid
movements you can't pull
your body away, this lucent
smooth sexual organ
ruffled underneath
like a swimming orchid,
offers you a second-
hand ecstasy, saying
you can only get
this close by being
separate, you can only
see this clearly
through a wall of glass,
only imagine
what it might be like
to succumb to something
beyond yourself,
becoming nothing
but that pulsing,
your whole being reduced
to the medusa,
tentacled tresses flowing
entangled in a slow-motion
whiplash of rapture –
while you stand there,
an onlooker
turning to stone.

The Cardinal Flower

After an afternoon
of no fish, no strikes, nothing
rising for the fly
you tied yourself
out of deer hair, squirrel tail,
and turkey feathers,
you begin to give up,
your attention drifting
on the river's rippled skin,
along its bubbling eddies,
down the spillways between
boulders rusted orange,
and into pools shot through
with sun, like amber beer.
You wouldn't mind one now,
and you start back,
working your way along
a rocky shoal the river
has strewn with still puddles
filmed with silver-blue
iridescent mirrors.
Maybe you'll try to catch
the evening in watercolors,
exchanging one bag
of supplies for another,
flies for fine-haired brushes
you'll dip in the very
river you're painting,
the reflected sunset like
the pink-fading-to-silver
stripe of a rainbow trout.
But that one too
is bound to get away,
the painting you imagine
always fading

The Cardinal Flower

into the one you put
on paper and will never
get right. And yet you like
to think of it as you
head home. And suddenly
there it is, startling you
with its scarlet blooms,
the cardinal flower
alone on the riverbank,
holding your gaze taut
as the hummingbird
its survival depends on,
one red touch of the brush
to focus the whole scene.

Car Radio

Alone on the highway, you're nowhere
and anywhere inside your car. Velocity
throws time out the window like a cigarette
that hits the road and explodes in sparks,
and this glass and steel sheath of speed
becomes a time machine whose control panel
is the digital radio. Pop oldies and
what they now call Classic Rock transport you
to high school dances in gyms and hotels,
rock concerts in hockey rinks, summer camp,
even the monkey bars on the playground.
Each song brings back a different time and place,
some of which you'd rather not revisit,
and much of the music is lousy, embarrassing,
but all you have to do is press the SEEK button
and you can escape to somewhere else:
an almost-forgotten sublet in a city
where you haven't lived for decades,
the rooftop of a Miami high-rise at night,
a restaurant on the other side of the world.
And then there are all those times in other cars,
and you feel the one you're in transmogrifying
into an old VW bug, a battered Ford van
during the epoch of eight tracks and FM converters,
a friend's souped-up Jeep, the monster station wagons
of the grade school car pool. Some songs hit you
with a surge of fervency almost as pure
as it used to be when you could briefly think
of your life as a movie with a good soundtrack,
singing along to it until you got hoarse.
You don't do that any more, you've lost
that dorky and impetuous intensity,
though sometimes you look down at the speedometer
and you're going 85, and certain songs
can almost make you weep for junior high

and the obsessive, hopeless crushes of that era.
It gets to be too much, though, too tiring,
memories fading in and out like stations,
each exerting its capricious, hankering demands
with no resolution, so in order to break the spell
of nostalgia you switch to a jazz station
at the far left of the dial, music that doesn't
tug unfairly at your emotions, that brings you back
to the present, to clouds streaking the blue sky
and a flock of starlings rising up and turning
all at once in flight like notes in harmony
or all those selves inside you coming together.

from Incomplete Knowledge (2006)

Fork

Because on the first day of class you said,
"In ten years most of you won't be writing,"
barely hiding that you hoped it would be true;
because you told me over and over, in front of the class,
that I was "hopeless," that I was wasting my time
but more importantly yours, that I *just didn't get it*;
because you violently scratched out every other word,
scrawled "Awk" and "Eek" in the margins
as if you were some exotic bird,
then highlighted your own remarks in pink;
because you made us proofread the galleys
of your how-I-became-a-famous-writer memoir;
because you wanted disciples, and got them,
and hated me for not becoming one;
because you were beautiful and knew it, and used it,
making wide come-fuck-me eyes
at your readers from the jackets of your books;
because when, at the end of the semester,
you grudgingly had the class over for dinner
at your over-decorated pseudo-Colonial
full of photographs with you at the center,
you served us take-out pizza on plastic plates
but had us eat it with your good silver;
and because a perverse inspiration rippled through me,

I stole a fork, slipping it into the pocket of my jeans,
then hummed with inward glee the rest of the evening
to feel its sharp tines pressing against my thigh
as we sat around you in your dark paneled study
listening to you blather on about your latest prize.
The fork was my prize. I practically sprinted
back to my dorm room, where I examined it:
a ridiculously ornate pattern, with vegetal swirls
and the curvaceous initials of one of your ancestors,
its flamboyance perfectly suited to your

105

Fork

red-lipsticked and silk-scarved ostentation.

That summer, after graduation, I flew to Europe,
stuffing the fork into one of the outer pouches
of my backpack. On a Eurail pass I covered ground
as only the young can, sleeping in youth hostels,
train stations, even once in the Luxembourg Gardens.
I'm sure you remember the snapshots you received
anonymously, each featuring your fork
at some celebrated European location: your fork
held at arm's length with the Eiffel Tower
listing in the background; your fork
in the meaty hand of a smiling Beefeater;
your fork balanced on Keats's grave in Rome
or sprouting like an antenna from Brunelleschi's dome;
your fork dwarfing the Matterhorn.
I mailed the photos one by one – if possible
with the authenticating postmark of the city
where I took them. It was my mission that summer.

That was half my life ago. But all these years
I've kept the fork, through dozens of moves
and changes – always in the same desk drawer
among my pens and pencils, its sharp points
spurring me on. It became a talisman
whose tarnished aura had as much to do
with me as you. You might even say your fork
made me a writer. Not you, your fork.
You are still the worst teacher I ever had.
You should have been fired but instead got tenure.
As for the fork, just yesterday my daughter
asked me why I keep a fork in my desk drawer,
and I realized I don't need it any more.
It has served its purpose. Therefore
I am returning it to you with this letter.

God's Penis

As usual, I had my zealous eye
on Nancy Morris, the object both of my desire
and my envy: Professor Schneider's pet
in Seminar on Jewish Mysticism,
the one he'd stop his lectures for to offer
some private suggestion about her thesis.
Her seriousness masked her blonde, smooth beauty
in frown lines I'd been trying to read between
all term: was she a Goody Two-shoes
or the sensualist I sometimes thought I glimpsed,
in the way, for instance, she was sucking
on her pen cap that day? I couldn't take
my eyes away, or keep my errant mind
from unbuttoning her cashmere cardigan.
But she, as always, had her blue-eyed attention,
her whole rapt being, focused on Schneider.
Was she in love with this hunched homunculus
older than his fifty years, almost a mystic himself,
who whispered quotations from Hassidic sages
in a German accent as thick as his gray beard?

During a lull in our discussion of the Kabbala
Schneider mentioned in passing an article
he'd seen in one of the scholarly journals
on God's penis. None of us had ever heard
anything crude pass through his oracular lips,
and before we knew whether to snicker
or take him at his startling word, his chosen pupil
gasped violently and bolted up like someone
suddenly possessed, with a force that sent
her chair clattering backwards. Everyone stared,
but she was speechless, grabbing at her neck.
"Are you choking?" I asked, remembering the pen cap,
and, as if this were a desperate game of charades,
she pointed at me – her first acknowledgment

of my existence. "Heimlich Maneuver!"
someone shouted, and Schneider lurched across the room,
and then he was doing it to her, hugging her from behind,
his hands clasped together under her snug breasts
and his pelvis pressing into her blue-jeaned ass,
closing his eyes and groaning with the exertion.

If it is true what Buber says, that no encounter
lacks a spiritual significance, then what
in God's unutterable name was this one
all about? Their long-awaited intimacy
nightmarishly fulfilled, or some excruciating twist
on "the sacrament of the present moment"? –
a phrase I remembered but couldn't have told you
where in the syllabus of mystic intimations
it came from. I couldn't have told you
anything: there was nothing but their dire embrace
wavering with the luminous surround
of a hallucination – and something inside me
rushing out toward them, silently pleading
"God, don't let her die!" The answer came,
torpedoing through the air and ricocheting
with a smack against the framed void of the blackboard.
Relief and embarrassment flooded the room
while the girl who had choked on God's penis
looked around astonished, as though she'd just returned
from a world beyond our knowing.

Saint

I find you where I found you years ago,
stone saint from fifteenth-century France
whom I can count on always to be here
in this church-like corner of the museum.

Forgive me for not visiting in so long.
Now I want to tell you everything
that has happened to me since I last saw you,
but I can see by your deeply shadowed eyes

that you already know. I place myself directly
in your warm and comprehending gaze.
I want to lose myself in the thick folds
of your stone robe, in the ripples of your beard.

The smooth dome of your bald head
is the firmament of your compassion.
Put down your heavy book and lay your hand
gently on top of my head. Pray for me.

from An Undertaking

for Andy, in memory

6. *His Socks*

Starting with the tumulus
on the floor beside his dresser,
clean but not yet put away
(now never to be put away),
a cairn of soft rocks
at least two feet high,
though many of them were not
balled up into pairs
but loose, or tied to their mates.
There were more in the dresser,
more on the closet shelves,
nests of them, like litters
of some small mammal, sleeping –
or dead, like the litter
of newborn rabbits that froze
when we were kids.
We buried them in a shoebox.
In every box my father
and I went through, no matter
what it contained – old papers,
framed photos, cassette tapes –
there would always be
at least a few more pairs,
and the one who found them
would call to the other,
"More socks," in sad amazement,
or exasperated bafflement,
because, for the life of us,
we couldn't find an explanation.
And what might have seemed
one of his endearing foibles
we couldn't keep from seeing

as some dark obsession,
one more thing about him
we hadn't known, would never
understand. Who could need
so many socks? Nylon dress socks,
gym socks of white cotton,
gray wool hunting socks
with an orange band on top,
even a few, from deep
in a trunk, with name tags
our mother had sewn in
decades ago. Enough socks
for several lifetimes,
though his one life was over.
Socks whose heels were worn
to a tenuous mesh, others
in their original packaging,
but most somewhere between.
If I'd taken them all I never
would have had to buy
another pair, no matter
how long I lived. But I
kept thinking of his feet
and how those socks would
never warm them again.
I took only a few pairs –
loose-fitting cotton, gray –
to wear to bed on cold nights,
my own feet sheathed
in the contours of his.

Visitation

for my mother

Walking past the open window, she is surprised
by the song of the white-throated sparrow
and stops to listen. She has been thinking of
the dead ones she loves – her father who lived
over a century, and her oldest son, suddenly gone
at forty-seven – and she can't help thinking
she has called them back, that they are calling her
in the voices of these birds passing through Ohio
on their spring migration ... because, after years
of summers in upstate New York, the white-throat
has become something like the family bird.
Her father used to stop whatever he was doing
and point out its clear, whistling song. She hears it
again: "Poor Sam Peabody Peabody Peabody."
She tries not to think, "Poor Andy," but she
has already thought it, and now she is weeping.
But then she hears another, so clear, it's as if
the bird were in the room with her, or in her head,
telling her that everything will be all right.
She cannot see them from her second-story window –
they are hidden in the new leaves of the old maple,
or behind the white blossoms of the dogwood –
but she stands and listens, knowing they will stay
for only a few days before moving on.

The Names of Things

Just after breakfast and still
waking up, I take the path cut
through the meadow, my mind caught
in some rudimentary stage,
the stems of timothy bending
inward with the weight of a single
drop of condensed fog clinging
to each of their fuzzy heads
that brush wetly against my jeans.
Out on a rise, the lupines stand
like a choir singing their purples,
pinks and whites to the buttercups
spread thickly through the grasses –
and to the sparser daisies, orange
hawkweed, pink and white clover,
purple vetch, butter-and-eggs.
It's a pleasure to name things
as long as one doesn't get
hung up about it. A pleasure, too,
to pick up the dirt road and listen
to my sneakers soaked with dew
scrunching on the damp pinkish sand –
that must be feldspar, an element
of granite, I remember from
fifth grade. I don't know what
this black salamander with yellow spots
is called – I want to say yellow-
spotted salamander, as if names
innocently sprang from things
themselves. Purple columbines
nod in a ditch, escapees
from someone's garden. It isn't
until I'm on my way back
that they remind me of the school
shootings in Colorado,

the association clinging to the spurs
of their delicate, complex blooms.
And I remember the hawk
in hawkweed, and that it's also
called devil's paintbrush, and how
lupines are named after wolves ...
how like second thoughts the darker
world encroaches even on these
fields protected as a sanctuary,
something ulterior always
creeping in like seeds carried
in the excrement of these buoyant
goldfinches, whose yellow bodies
are as bright as joy itself,
but whose species name in Latin
means "sorrowful."

Index of Titles and First Lines

A Note About the Author

Jeffrey Harrison is the author of four books of poetry, *The Singing Underneath* (1988), selected by James Merrill for the National Poetry Series, *Signs of Arrival* (1996), *Feeding the Fire* (2001), and *Incomplete Knowledge,* forthcoming in fall 2006 from Four Way Books (New York). His chapbook *An Undertaking* was published in 2005. He has received fellowships from the John Simon Guggenheim Memorial Foundation and the National Endowment for the Arts, as well as two Pushcart Prizes, the Amy Lowell Traveling Poetry Scholarship, and the Lavan Younger Poets Award from the Academy of American Poets. His poems have appeared in *The New Yorker, The New Republic, Poetry, The Paris Review, The Yale Review, Poets of the New Century,* and in many other magazines and anthologies. He has taught at several universities and schools, including George Washington University, Phillips Academy, where he was the Roger Murray Writer-in-Residence, and College of the Holy Cross. He is currently on the faculty of the Stonecoast MFA Program at the University of Southern Maine.

Other Books from Waywiser

*Expanded UK edition